COVENTRY
THEN & NOW

BRITAIN IN OLD PHOTOGRAPHS

COVENTRY
THEN & NOW

DAVID MCGRORY

The
History
Press

To the people of Coventry, old and new.

First published 2011

The History Press
The Mill, Brimscombe Port
Stroud, Gloucestershire, GL5 2QG
www.thehistorypress.co.uk

British Library Cataloguing in Publication Data.
A catalogue record for this book is available from the British Library.

ISBN 978 0 7524 5994 3

Typesetting and origination by The History Press
Production managed by Jellyfish Print Solutions and manufactured in India

CONTENTS

ACKNOWLEDGEMENTS

Special thanks to Rob Orland for all his hard work with helping to supply, take and prepare photographs. Also special thanks to Rob's son, Steve Orland, who took some excellent photos for this book. Those with an interest in Coventry should visit Rob's excellent website www.historiccoventry.co.uk.

I would also like to thank Tony Rose, PC Charlotte Godfrey and West Midlands Police, John Ashby, Trevor Pring, CV One, Paul Gilroy, Sue Atkins, Andrew Mealey and Coventry Local Studies.

INTRODUCTION

Historically, Coventry has developed much like any other city in England; spurts of growth through the medieval period made it a powerful walled city. The growth continued through the fifteenth and sixteenth centuries at least up to the Dissolution in 1539, when with the fall of the priory came a drop in population. The great priory cathedral of St Mary became a literal builder's yard as the building from its roof to its floor tiles was dismantled. Much was sold by its new owners and the rest was scavenged by locals. Even by the late nineteenth century parts of the great building were being discovered, forming many things from fireplaces to garden harbours.

By the seventeenth century, the city remained unchanged, packed with timbered buildings, straggling narrow lanes and still sitting safely within its strong embattled wall. This wall, which had defied King Charles the First in 1642, fell in 1662 to his restored son King Charles the Second. The slighting of the wall in more peaceable times fell to Lord Compton and 500 men, who began the demolition symbolically at New Gate, Charles the First's attack point in 1642. After the slighting, Coventry sat open within the shattered and scattered remnants of its wall. No doubt much of the stonework was sold off and again scavenged by locals.

Eighteenth-century Coventry didn't move much. Described in 1702 as having buildings 'mostly of timber work and old', it felt more like a small market town. Little building work took place, just brick cottages, few of which survive. Later in the century most chose to reface old timbered buildings with new modern brick façades; this can still be seen in much of what survives in Hay Lane and the Burges. A small number of larger gentlemen's residences were built in Little Park Street and Hill Top. The only significant civic building of the eighteenth century was the County Hall, with its adjoining gaol built in the latter half of 1776. This replaced an older gaol on the site. The County Hall continued as a courtroom until the early 1980s and has since stood empty for ten years awaiting the fate of most historic buildings these days, to be turned into a bar/restaurant. At least it will survive, unlike some historic buildings within the city bounds that have been destroyed by bored youths. Modern youth is not the only problem, for in the past our own council has put paid to many an ancient building. Luckily now we live in slightly more enlightened times. This does not, however, stop the odd one slipping through.

In 1812 Coventry experienced its first major change to its street plans; a local tradition states that this was due to the Prince Regent. When in 1807 the prince's carriage entered the city from the south, the entrance was then through the narrow and congested Warwick/Greyfriars Lane. Apparently, despite his importance the prince was stuck for some time in the lane and later was said to have stated that he hoped things would improve on his next visit. It did, for when he next passed through in 1815 he was quickly driven along the wider thoroughfare we know as Hertford Street. The prince was duly impressed.

The first major destruction and rebuilding in the city happened in 1820, when the west side of Broadgate was taken down. This was done to enlarge the market area, which had previously been narrow, and to improve the vista. This side of Broadgate was timbered with houses dating back to the fourteenth century. With them fell the sixteenth-century Mayor's Parlour, with its pillared doorway and balcony clock, with figures in red and green striking the hours. This was the Mayor's official office, where he met and greeted and also dispensed justice.

The next major work in the city was for the building of Hales Street, which was opened in 1848. This occurred after the in-filling of the Mill Dam, a large sheet of water which lay here. There were, however, no buildings between St Agnes Lane and the Grammar School, as this formed the school's play area. Many small, isolated building projects took place throughout the rest of the nineteenth century, including the enlarging of the market square off Broadgate and the building of a market hall with its landmark 100ft-tall clock tower. Other work included the demolition of timbered houses below St Mary's Hall and the building of a new police station and courts.

Into the twentieth century and a whole block of ancient buildings were demolished around 1903 to eventually build the present Council House; the work for which started in 1913, finished in 1917 and led to it being officially opened in 1920. The old buildings originally stood further forward than the present council house, and, buried below the pavement, in-filled, are a number of medieval cellars. This was followed in 1929 by the removal of hundreds of buildings to create Corporation Street. One surviving image of this reminds one of the aftermath of the Blitz.

Perhaps the most devastating pre-war change to the city was in 1936, with the total demolition of a number of Coventry's most loved ancient streets, namely Butcher Row, the Bull Ring, Little Butcher Row and other nearby thoroughfares. If it had survived, this area would have mirrored the Shambles in York. But then the powers that be decided it was a slum and it had to go. Besides, the motor car could then get into Broadgate quicker, but at what cost? It was around this time that the city architects began to envisage a more modern city with wider roads. Donald Gibson was taken on as city architect, and more plans lay ahead involving the demolition of most of the old centre and the widening of many of the central roads. Coventry was about to have its old heart ripped out, then came the bombs and the changes keep coming!

David McGrory, 2011

THE CATHEDRAL QUARTER

THE PILGRIM'S REST in Palmer Lane, from a nineteenth-century engraving. Although not in the Cathedral Quarter, the Pilgrim's Rest had close connections, being the guesthouse for pilgrims visiting Coventry Priory. A rebuilt inn – with parts dating to the fourteenth century – it was knocked down in 1936.

LOOKING DOWN THE side of Holy Trinity Church, *c.* 1926. Dovecote House is on the left and the top of Butcher Row is on the right. Dovecote House dated to around the sixteenth century and the gable on the right had a triangle of square holes for doves to go in and out, hence the name. The smaller white building on the left was, for many years, a butcher shop.

Today the view bears no resemblance. Holy Trinity Church, thankfully, remains on the left and ahead is Primark, which began life as Owen Owen. On the left are flats built to the rear of Cathedral Lanes shopping centre in 1990. Unlike in the past, very few people actually live in the city centre itself.

THIS PAINTING LOOKS from the top of Butcher Row along the Spicerstoke, towards Holy Trinity Church. Spicerstoke took its name from the medieval spice merchants who once lived and traded here. The painting gives the impression that the lane was wider than it was; it certainly wouldn't have been easily accessed by a coach.

The present view conveys the narrowness of the lane, and the flats jut out into part of the area once occupied by Dovecote House. The frontage of Holy Trinity Church is no longer hidden, as it was up to 1936.

11

UP THE LANE by Holy Trinity Church, photographed around 1920. On the right stands the Free Library, opened in 1871 and paid for by John Gulson and Samuel Carter. Gulson also paid for an extension, opened in 1890, and in 1917 it was renamed the Gulson Library. It was still in use until about 1988 and, although it managed to survive the Blitz, it fell to planners building Cathedral Lanes shopping centre.

The leafiness, spire and cobbles are still pleasant today. Those who walk down here are unaware that they are walking over burials still present from when the churchyard extended nearly to the gaol wall.

LOOKING ACROSS PRIORY Row towards Lychgate Cottage, *c.* 1912. The cottage was built on the west entrance of the Cathedral of St Mary in 1650 by the Reverend John Bryan, late treasurer of the Parliamentarian army and vicar of Holy Trinity Church, using re-used timbers which had previously been stored in the churchyard. His own house, Tower House, was built over the transepts near Hilltop. On the right is the original Blue Coat School.

Still a pleasant view today, little has changed except for the fact that the original Tudor corner cottages into the Bull Ring have been replaced with a mock Tudor building, built in 1937 for Timothy Whites the chemist.

THIS PHOTOGRAPH, TAKEN around 1860 from Holy Trinity churchyard, shows the backs of the houses which fronted Butcher Row. The frontage of Holy Trinity Church was originally open in early medieval times, overlooking a large market square. This, over time, was in-filled with Great and Little Butcher Row and the Bull Ring. Between the church and buildings ran the very narrow Trinity Lane.

The view today gives an idea of the medieval perspective, pre-Butcher Row, with the trees once again adding to the pleasant view.

THE BLUECOAT SCHOOL for girls was rebuilt over its original site in 1856. During this work, the west entrance to the priory cathedral of St Mary was exposed and built into the new building. The girls received a three-year education at the school, with one year boarding. Sitting within its beautiful main hall they learned the 'Three Rs' and the art of housekeeping, as deemed essential to the Victorian lady.

This is probably one of Coventry's most unusual buildings, a fine prospect thankfully unchanged. In 1999-2000, the burial ground was removed and the main site of the priory church was excavated. The pillars of the west entrance are now almost totally exposed, as is part of the main church and the undercroft. There is also the visitor centre, with excellent staff.

THE UNSTABLENESS OF Holy Trinity's tower led to the building of this wooden campanile in the mid-nineteenth century. The bells were rung to celebrate victory in the Crimea so vigorously that the tower itself swayed from side to side and was in danger of collapse. All uses afterwards were at a more subdued rate and the tower survived into the 1960s.

The same view today, taken from Holy Trinity churchyard. The campanile had stood in the new Trinity burial ground opposite. Although not large, amazingly it held over 4,000 burials, all of which have since been removed during the excavation of the priory. It was noted that the deeper burials actually sat on the cathedral floor.

THE REAR OF Holy Trinity Church, *c.* 1912. The original Priory Row did not follow this straight route but curved behind Holy Trinity to the old Bishop's Palace, which survived into the nineteenth century, divided into tenements. The spire of Holy Trinity, which was restored in recent years, had previously collapsed in 1665, killing a small child and badly damaging part of the building.

Today Priory Row is shorter due to the building of the new cathedral. The older Priory Row continued as a straight lane into Priory Street, but now it ends at the entrance to the cathedral's café.

17

ST MICHAEL'S AVENUE, running along the north side of St Michael, then still a parish church, *c.* 1910. On the left, beyond the bollards, stands a later replacement for the gravestone of John Parkes. Known as Parkes the Invincible, he was an eighteenth-century gladiator who fought with the short sword or flail. After fighting 350 matches throughout Europe, Parkes returned home, dying in Coventry aged fifty-two in 1733.

The view today looks relatively unchanged, except for the fact that the new cathedral now stands on the left of the walk. Parkes still lies here, his white headstone noticed by few except for the squirrels who delight tourists with their over-friendliness.

LOOKING DOWN PEPPER Lane (formerly Gaol Lane), *c*. 1910. The Toby's Head, which stands on the right, was destroyed by a high explosive on 14 November 1940. Apparently, when the site was being cleared two years later, twenty barrels of beer were unearthed in the cellar. On the left are various shops, leading down to the prison governor's residence attached to Coventry Gaol.

Apart from the Governor's House, the tower and spire of St Michael, and the timbered Golden Cross on the right, nothing survived the bombs of 14 November 1940. Pepper Lane is now little more than a taxi rank and delivery point for Wilkinson.

A PHOTOGRAPH TAKEN from the tower of St Michael in the 1950s. The old castle ditch runs under the tower and follows the broad walk down the centre, coming out of the chancel and apse. Beyond lay New Street, said to have been created by the builders of the church in the fourteenth century.

Coventry University was built over New Street in the early 1960s. Work continues in the distance on the right. This building site recently revealed a Roman ditch, dated by pottery and a brooch. Coventry has a far older past than most think.

COVENTRY CATHEDRAL, DESIGNED by Sir Basil Spence, took eight years to build, beginning in 1954, with the foundation stone being laid by HM the Queen in 1956, and finally consecrated in 1962. In 1999 it was voted Britain's best-loved building. The building has recently introduced an entrance charge, which has had a significant effect on visitor numbers.

The completed building cost £1,385,000, and in its first year received two and a half million visitors through its majestic pillared and glass-fronted entrance. The present entrance for coach parties is, strangely, through the back door.

A VIEW FROM the tower of St Michael in the 1930s. In the foreground is the High Street and beyond is Little Park Street, with Bushell's at the end. Before the tower of Christchurch, still then attached to its second re-built church, is the Central Post Office sorting depot, which was still in use in the 1980s. Noticeable by their absence are the office blocks and towers.

The same view today minus the Post Office sorting depot and Bushell's. What stands out most is the modern idea that everything built must be a box and new boxes must be glass – useful as workplaces but visually inadequate, adding nothing to the cityscape. Perhaps a Gherkin would help!

ANOTHER VIEW TAKEN from the tower, looking north-west. Beyond the new buildings lining Trinity Street and the Hippodrome, the city seems to quickly disappear into leafy suburbs. The tallest building in Coventry at that time was the tower and spire of St Michael, our highest resident the weathercock.

More boxes, the tower blocks were built in the late 1960s. The brown building (mid-ground) was until recently the Post Office sorting centre. It is presently up for sale as sorting is done many miles away. For the first time since the introduction of the stamp, the city no longer deals with its own post. Interestingly, the higher portion of the Trinity Street block was reduced to bring the whole building into line.

THE INTERIOR OF the parish church of St Michael in 1905, said by Sir Christopher Wren to be a masterpiece and is indeed a thing of beauty and magnificence. The origins of this church lie in a small chapel around the south aisle area, known as the chapel of St Michael in the Bailey. It was the Earl of Chester's chapel within the bailey of Coventry Castle. It grew massively from the late fourteenth century to become the building we see now.

The original parish church of St Michael became a cathedral in 1918, and, although it still has a subdued beauty, it is a sad reflection on its previous magnificence. If anything, the church's significance now is its symbolism, not only of the destruction and futility of war but also of reconciliation.

THE APSE OF the old cathedral showing the Adelaide window, some of which is now in Iceland, and the apparently Victorian tiled floor, not the flagstones we see today. The apse, although simple, has a strange beauty with its magnificent tall windows.

The apse today gives little away; it is striking because of its starkness, which works with the simplicity of the charred cross. The cross was created by the cathedral stonemason, Jock Forbes, on the morning of 15 November, when the cathedral lay in ruins. He tied together two charred beams with a piece of wire and stood it amongst the rubble. This one is a fibreglass copy.

THE LADY CHAPEL photographed in 1912, nicknamed the 'Chapel on the Mount' because of its great height standing above what was the church's charnel house, which was full of excess bones and skulls from the churchyard. The fourteenth-century stalls in the chapel held some of the finest carvings in the church. Sadly, none survived.

Today, again somewhat stark, the chapel is more striking because we can see what it was like before. Bishop Yeatman-Biggs's fine effigy now stands where the altar used to. Biggs was the first bishop of the church as a cathedral. Note that the third window on the left is now the entrance from the new cathedral.

LOOKING TOWARDS THE apse and Lady Chapel shortly after 14 November 1940. People wander the ruins in disbelief. The steel straps lie twisted on the floor; these are from the 1882 restoration. They were supposed to help support the roof; in fact they helped to bring it down, pulling and twisting in the heat until it collapsed.

The same view today, the cathedral floor flagged and concreted over, including the old inscribed burial slabs. The canopy joining the old and new can be seen on the left.

LOOKING TOWARDS THE west entrance and north aisle, containing (far right) the Girdlers' Chapel, last resting place of Sir Skears Rew, the second only Coventry mayor to be knighted. It was above the north aisle that incendiaries first took hold, setting the roof alight, while those who fought the fires were occupied on the south aisle. From here Coventry Cathedral burned.

The view today is missing the dividing columns and top windows, which brought streams of coloured light into the building.

A NICE VIEW from around 1910, looking up St Michael's Avenue towards Holy Trinity Church. This leafy lane was a favoured promenade for many Coventrians. It was along this lane, before the north door (left), that one of the vicars of St Michael's Church used to take potshots at a ghostly monk who walked here.

Below we see the grand porch of the old and new, symbolically joining the two buildings together.

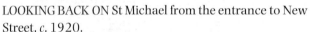

LOOKING BACK ON St Michael from the entrance to New Street, *c.* 1920.

What were once roads are now an open square with large grey granite balls. In the foreground through much of the summer is a water feature, which although not spectacular brings pleasure to young children who like to run through it. Off picture to the left is the Herbert, home to the city's museum, art and archives.

A BEAUTIFUL ENGRAVING showing the splendour that was the old cathedral around 1860. Also of interest is the huge graveyard, which originally ran down to the Sherbourne and across to the present site of Coventry University, which still has gravestones in its grounds.

The same view today with only the apse area showing. The new cathedral, however, looks quite striking from this angle with its huge entrance, sheer sides, windows, and Epstein's bronze of St Michael and the Devil.

LOOKING ACROSS THE outside of the apse of St Michael on a winter's day in 1906. Beyond can be seen the last house in Priory Row. Beyond this lay the original Triumph factory.

Today, the most noticeable changes are the tree and the student accommodation block on the right. Coventry University is particularly noted for its engineering and design section; it also has a very large contingent of foreign students.

LOOKING UP BAYLEY Lane, *c.* 1910. St Michael's south porch, which is the site of the earliest chapel, can be seen jutting out. On the left is Draper's Hall, once home of the Draper's Company. Draper's was a very popular venue in the eighteenth and nineteenth centuries for plays and balls. The building has an untouched Georgian ballroom and awaits restoration. Above it, up until 1852, stood a row of timbered cottages.

The view today is practically unchanged, except for the fact that the glass is gone from the cathedral windows.

LOOKING DOWN BAYLEY Lane, *c.* 1910. Number 22, on the right, dates back to the seventeenth century and has been a baker's shop, a curio shop, then, for most of the twentieth century, a solicitor's. Underneath the building is a surprisingly large cellar. Beyond can be seen St Mary's Hall. The nooks below the north window once contained images of Henry VI and his ancestors, matching the window above.

The only change in the scene is the ruined cathedral. One unnoticeable but significant change is that about 20ft of the road was raised around ten years ago to make the hall easily accessible for wheelchairs, covering the two steps which were previously at the entrance. The frontage of the hall was not always cobbled; in the nineteenth century the road was made up of wooden blocks to dampen passing noise.

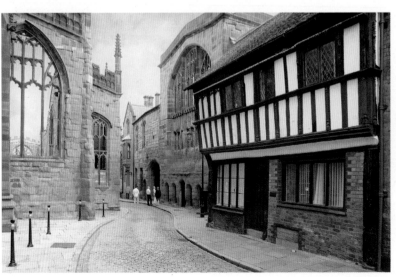

A PHOTOGRAPH BY the late Arthur Cooper, taken in 1936 and looking south in the Great Hall of St Mary's. The Guild of St Mary started the hall in 1340; it later grew, becoming the Guild of the Holy Trinity. This guild was responsible for the hall as we see it today. The armour of the Minstrels Gallery is all that remains of the city armoury. The helmet on the central suit is the noted 15th Coventry Sallet.

The hall today. Four of the full-size portraits are now missing; they are stored away in the Herbert as they are in poor condition. The six remaining ones in the hall were restored about ten years ago. The hall is still one of the most visited places in the city today and is considered to be one of the finest guildhalls in England.

LOOKING NORTH DOWN the Great Hall, *c.* 1905. The large chandeliers, or electroliers, replaced the earlier Francis Skidmore gas chandeliers. One of the councillors at the time complained, saying that they made the hall look like the Rover Car Showrooms at the bottom of Hertford Street. As the use of electricity was still fairly new, a feature of the lights was their large exposed light bulbs.

The same view today, minus the electric chandeliers and with the restored Victorian lights. The north window dates to the late fifteenth century and depicts Henry VI and his ancestors. It was designed to go with the Coventry Tapestry below, which shows Henry VI and Margaret of Anjou, and forms one of the last major vestiges of the cult of Henry VI left in England.

THE GOLDEN CROSS, photographed in 1914. The Cross, a fifteenth-century building, was heavily restored in the nineteenth century. Part of the wood used included the old bell frame from nearby St Michael's. This probably came about as the inn was the watering hole for the church's bell ringers. On the left can be seen the corner of the Baptist Church of St Michael, which was destroyed on 14 November 1940.

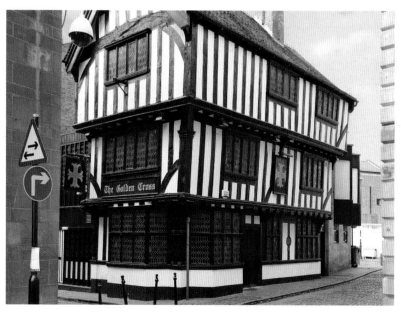

The inn has changed little today, at least on the outside. The inside, however, is now painted a number of interesting, or, as one could say, challenging colours. The Golden Cross takes its name from the tradition that Coventry's ancient mint stood here, or was within this building, when Edward IV's new gold and silver light coinage was struck here in 1465.

THE COUNTY HALL, dating from 1869. The hall was built under the guidance of Alderman John Hewitt, Coventry's mayor and most noted magistrate and thief taker. Completed in 1776, it was attached to the city gaol. The entrance to the right of the building was the Lodge Gate. It was from here that the condemned mounted a cart, which carried them with their coffin to the gallows on Whitley Common.

Today the exterior remains little changed, having lain empty for ten years. Much of the old building, including its court room, has now been stripped out, with plans to turn it into a pub restaurant. Some of the internal features have, however, been left, including the judge's chair.

2

SPON STREET
TO JORDAN WELL

THE COUNCIL HOUSE in the High Street on 7 September 1946, and a military bypass for the 'Burma Comes to Britain' exhibition to raise money for the Army Benevolent Fund.

LOOKING UP SPON Street from the corner of Lower Holyhead Road in the 1930s. The junction in the foreground is the point where stage coaches entered the street when the Holyhead Road was opened. Many coaches took this corner too quickly, sending drivers, passengers, and coach and horses crashing into the ground. In the background can be seen the old Rudge Works, once the largest manufacturer of cycles in the world.

In the 1970s it was decided to preserve what was left of Spon Street, and, amongst its surviving medieval buildings, others were rebuilt, such as the Green Dragon from Much Park. It is said that Spon Street now has more fourteenth-century Wealden houses than any street in England. As you can see, some town planner has thoughtfully placed his tower block halfway down the street, destroying the perspective.

40

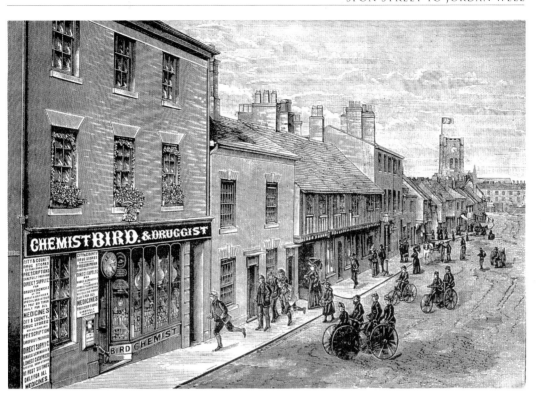

A LATE NINETEENTH-CENTURY engraving looking down Spon Street towards St John the Baptist Church. On the left is Bird's the chemist and druggist. The assistant chemist here, a Londoner named Arthur Devereux, was hanged in 1905 by Albert Pierrepoint for murdering his wife and two children. Beyond is the original Fairfax Charity School, followed by a nice row of Tudor shops.

Today, the Rising Sun pub stands on most of the site of Bird's, and the Fairfax Club now resides within the later rebuilt Fairfax School with its double apex. There is a gap where the Tudor shops once stood.

41

THE OLD WINDMILL Inn is said to be the oldest inn in Coventry, photographed around 1930 when Sydney Brown became licensee. After his death in 1940, his wife Ann took over the pub, and thereafter under her the pub was often referred to as Ma Brown's. The pub stayed in the Brown family until 1975.

Today it remains one of the best-loved pubs in the city, serving good beer and full of character. Interestingly, this Tudor building was originally divided into two, with the present entrance acting as the entrance to a flagged courtyard, which separated the two houses. Beneath the stucco lies timber framing. The Windmill didn't actually become a pub until the early twentieth century, so the oldest inn in constant use in the city is the Golden Cross.

COURT NO. 38, KNOWN as Dyer's Arms Yard, photographed around 1957. Courts such as these, with their eighteenth-century cottage-style houses, were once common, not only in Spon Street

but throughout the city. Most had shared outside toilets and pumps. By 1957 they probably had a single tap over a Belfast sink. My own father was born in a similar court in nearby Hill Street.

Considering that this was once the most common form of housing in the city, practically nothing remains today. This remnant of a court today in Spon Street is currently partly occupied and is also home to the Coventry Watch Museum. Spon Street was once one of the centres of the Coventry watch trade.

BOND'S HOSPITAL AND Bablake School from an engraving published in 1869. Bond's was founded in 1507 by ex-Mayor Thomas Bond for ten poor men. Bond stipulated that the inmates wear hooded black gowns and attend daily matins, mass and evensong in nearby St John's to pray for the souls of Bond, his father and grandfather, and all Christian souls.

Relatively unchanged today, the chimneys, however, are new as most were blown off during the Blitz. The tree in the background in the old picture is the same tree, which stands today just in front of the old Bablake School, which was first mentioned when John Bedull was master in 1522. In 1560, Thomas Wheatley left a bequest to the school, but did not found it as tradition states.

BABLAKE SCHOOL AND Bond's Hospital from Hill Street, taken around 1905. Straddling the road just before the last apex once stood Hill Street Gate, one of the city's minor gates.

The scene on the left remains relatively unchanged today. The buildings are well looked after and in the roadway itself is now marked the site of the old gate which was excavated in recent years. A recent dig to the right, off Bond Street, unearthed the old wall ditch, which contained many late medieval leather shoes in remarkable condition.

A WINGRAVE TAKEN in the 1860s showing the church of St John the Baptist. In 1344 Queen Isabella gave a parcel of land here to build a chapel. Here she requested that prayers be said for the royal family and her late murdered husband, King Edward II. It was controlled by the Trinity Guild up until 1547. Its use then varied from a prison for Royalists in 1647 to a storehouse. It reopened as a parish church in 1734.

Still a beautiful church today with its embattled tower, which looks much smaller than it actually is. The church stands in what is now a very short Fleet Street. Fleet means to float, and with this in mind the church was built on oak piles above the ancient lake bed. Even today the church is still sitting just 1ft above water.

A BUSY FLEET Street leading onto the bottom of Smithford Street in 1912. The buildings to the left run into Hill Street; these were demolished when Corporation Street was built. In the distance up Smithford Street can be seen the spires of Trinity and St Michael. None of the buildings have survived.

Apart from a bit of churchyard wall, the view now is totally different. Fleet Street/Smithford Street ran to the left of the present white tower block. The first building opposite is the original corner building of Corporation Street and Fleet Street from the 1930s. Interestingly, the lamp post is a modern copy of the original.

A PHOTOGRAPH TAKEN in the early 1950s, showing the last building on Fleet Street, the City Arms. Across West Orchard Lane is the first building in Smithford Street, the Coventry Co-op, then minus its upper floors due to bomb damage. Both of these buildings were demolished to make way for the Lower Precinct.

The same view today taken from the corner of the Lower Precinct; the scene could hardly be any more different. Although the Lower Precinct was covered in recent years, it still retains many of its original 1950s' features, such as the cut-out balcony rail and picture lights.

A PHOTOGRAPH TAKEN on 25 May 1962 during the royal visit of the Queen to consecrate the New Cathedral. Here the crowds welcome Princess Margaret and Lord Snowdon, walking with the Lord Mayor Arthur Waugh up the original yellow and black tile-lined ramp from the Lower Precinct.

Today one can appreciate how much wider the entrance into the glass-roofed Lower Precinct is. Interestingly, below the area between the bottom of the ramp and the round café still runs the River Sherbourne. Here, in 1928, an otter emerged and was killed in Smithford Street.

THE REMAINS OF Smithford Street in 1954. Barratt's shoe shop and E. Palmer, pork butcher, had recently closed, awaiting their demolition for the building of Smithford Way. In the background can be seen the newly finished Marks & Spencer building, which was the first store to be built in the Upper Precinct.

A contrasting view today with trees, people and the round fountain, a fairly recent addition to this crossing point. Few in the modern scene would realise that only fifty odd years ago here they would have been strolling through a shoe shop and butcher's.

LOOKING DOWN THE Upper Precinct and along Smithford Street, running down to St John's, in 1954. The White Lion (right) still stands next to Marks & Spencer. This was the second inn of the site. Here, in 1734, Susannah Wall and her daughter were murdered by Susannah's nephew, Thomas Wildley, who was hanged for his crime. HMV now stands on the rear of the site.

The completed scene today. City architect Donald Gibson's precinct was the first pedestrian precinct in Britain; the idea, however, had originated with city engineer Ernest Ford. Gibson was later followed by Arthur Ling, who added the tower blocks.

A PHOTOGRAPH BY chemist Joseph Wingrave, looking from Broadgate into Smithford Street and the corner of Hertford Street in the 1860s. Behind the top-hatted policeman is the Coventry Hotel. Opposite in the corner shop window can be seen Peeping Tom, peeping from a niche in the former shop of Thomas Sharp, hatter and Coventry historian. Below this shop can be seen the King's Head hotel.

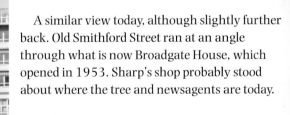

A similar view today, although slightly further back. Old Smithford Street ran at an angle through what is now Broadgate House, which opened in 1953. Sharp's shop probably stood about where the tree and newsagents are today.

LOOKING DOWN THE High Street towards Smithford Street, *c.* 1933. On the left is the arched entrance of the National Bank, later Lloyds Bank. Across Greyfriars Lane stands the pillared National Westminster Bank, opened in 1930. Beyond the NatWest is the later King's Head, opened Christmas 1879. Opposite stands the Burton's building and in the right foreground a fine Tudor house.

Today, the left-hand side remains relatively unchanged up to NatWest. Broadgate House now forms the backdrop instead of the King's Head, and on the right Cathedral Lanes takes the place of Burton's, although Burton's lay more between the bank and the present Godiva statue.

LOOKING UP THE High Street from the corner of Earl Street and Hay Lane around 1905. The late Victorian shops on the right survived; the corner shop was, through most of the twentieth century, a furniture shop and more recently a pub. Note the words painted on the large Elizabethan house on the left, 'Luckman's Wonder Pianos.' There is also a painted Luckman's sign on a building near the bottom of Hertford Street.

The view today bears the same perspective but relates little to the older view. This isn't helped by the fact that the building on the right is boarded up for refurbishment. Although this building still retains a Victorian look, not a lot of the original Victorian façade has survived.

LOOKING DOWN EARL Street into Gosford Street in the 1920s. The Council House stands on the left and beyond it stands Wheelers, giving an idea of how the road ran narrower. The Council House itself sits further back than the original road line. Very few images survive showing the left-hand side of Jordan Well, a street lined with buildings dating back to the fifteenth century.

Looking today past the Council House, with its bridge and Civic Centre 1 on the right. Beyond the Council House now stands Brown's, which was built on the old toilet block which began life before the war as the first stage of a museum funded by Sir Alfred Herbert. Beyond the present Brown's now stands the extended Herbert Art Gallery & Museum, started in the late 1950s.

LOOKING UP JORDAN Well, *c*. 1910. Hidden amongst these shops are many timbered buildings, some plastered over with late eighteenth- early nineteenth-century façades in an attempt to modernise them. The narrow gap on the right is the entrance to Freeth Street, which led into New Street. Both roads are now gone.

Today, nothing remains of the buildings in Jordan Well; the only recognisable feature is the tower of the Council House. Interestingly, the angle change (left) in the pavement survived; this marks the site of the actual well, which gave the street its name.

3

BISHOP STREET TO COVENTRY STATION

LOOKING DOWN THE bottom of Hertford Street, *c.* 1955. The taller buildings on the left still stand; the other, temporary shops, were replaced when Hertford Street was rebuilt as a pedestrian area. The temporary W.H. Smith's on the left was rebuilt on the same site and remained there until the 1990s.

LOOKING DOWN BISHOP Street, *c.* 1912. With the mix of ancient buildings tumbling down the hill and the spires, this makes for a fine view. Many of these houses were centuries older than their brick façades suggest. Hidden behind them were many fine timbered courtyards.

Unfortunately, nothing of the old street apart from the Grammar School has survived. The spires have also been interfered with by the erection of yet another tower block; this looks even worse from further up the street.

THE BOTTOM OF Bishop Street, taken around 1902. The Grammar School, with its adjoining building, still stands out and appears relatively well kept. The buildings on the left appear to be Victorian and apart from two refaced timbered buildings across the road, most appear to be Georgian. Tram lines can be seen in the street and it was here that the first steam-powered trams struggled to gain the hill.

The modern scene has little or nothing to commend it; boxes on the left, and the site of the last surviving Georgian house in the street demolished within the last two years, despite its age. The boarded-up area, now overgrown, awaits development sometime in the future. The last Georgian house was known by many as the Parson's Nose fish and chip shop.

LOOKING FROM THE Burges into Hales Street in 1910. Ahead is the old Grammar School, originally the twelfth-century chapel of the Hospital of St John, a refuge for sick wayfarers. In 1522, it housed three priests, three clerks and five sisters, maintaining thirty beds for the poor, which lined the chapel walls. In 1544 it was surrendered, and acquired by John Hales who converted it into a school

Although some of the scene survives, it is noticeable how an over-abundance of modern plain street furniture spoils the view. There are also other problems here, more boxes, and the fact that the old Grammar School is still boarded up, empty for more years than I can remember. The building is sadly still considered to be at risk.

LOOKING UP THE Burges into Cross Cheaping in 1931. Previously known as St John's Bridges, here two bridges crossed; the Sherbourne and Radford Brook. Burges simply means, in the old local dialect, Bridges. This was the narrowest point of the ancient Babbu Lacu, a lake which filled the central valley. In the Norman period a ferryman worked here, and Roman coins and objects have been unearthed.

Much of the bottom of the street remains, although the top end was demolished in 1936. The Tally Ho on the right was built around 1930 and is now called the Tudor Rose. It is hard to believe that the River Sherbourne crosses here, just to the side of the Coventry Cross pub. Many of the buildings on the left have later façades and some probably date back to the seventeenth century or earlier.

THE BOTTOM OF Cross Cheaping around 1912, marked by the little window box jutting out of the Talbot Inn on the corner of West Orchard. Beyond runs the Burges. The Talbot is named after John Talbot, Earl of Shrewsbury, known as the English Achilles. Jutting out beyond the ancient Talbot Inn are two large sixteenth-century merchants' houses. Most of the upper end of the street was demolished in 1936.

The entrance to the present West Orchards shopping complex is to the left and the upper part of the street bears little resemblance to the old street. Instead of continuing straight up, the road has, since 1953, swept around the Owen Owen building.

A WINGRAVE PHOTOGRAPH looking into Broadgate on market day in the 1860s. The last ever market held here was on 2 December 1867. After this the vendors traded from the newly built market hall. Waterloo House, on the right, was previously the site of the Old Mayor's Parlour. Above it is the Castle Hotel; one of its noted guests was Charles Dickens, who was presented with a Coventry watch.

The view today with Cathedral Lanes on the left and, in the foreground, a cobbled remnant of the old 1950s' island Broadgate, a nice reminder of the past in these modern surrounds.

A CAR GLIDING into Hertford Street in the 1950s. The clock strikes three and the fairly new Godiva and Peeping Tom figures, carved by Trevor Tennant, do their thing, an event which still amuses visitors today. The bridge area above the road originally contained the Bridge Restaurant, which had excellent views over Broadgate.

Hertford Street was pedestrianised in the late 1960s. The mechanism for the clock was created by Coventry watchmaker Edward Thomas Loseby in 1869/70. Loseby was so confident on its accuracy that he agreed to be fined £1 for every second it lost. The bronze bell that strikes the hours originally struck the hours with Loseby's clock in the old market clock tower, which was demolished in 1942.

LOOKING FROM HERTFORD Street into Broadgate, *c.* 1912. The car is parked outside the King's Head Hotel and beyond lies the Coventry Hotel. The width of old Broadgate can be appreciated; before 1820 it was much narrower. The Vaults pub across Broadgate has a wonderful wall painting of a windmill, representing Cheshire Ales. The gap between this and the next building took you into Butcher Row.

The same view today; in fact, the right-hand side of Broadgate would lie in the front of Cathedral Lanes, about where the glass roof is. The newsagent's under the clock has served the city for a number of years and is one of the few places in the city where you can buy a Godiva figure as a souvenir.

LOOKING DOWN HERTFORD Street, *c.* 1890. Most of the top of the street at this point was taken up by the Johnson & Mason building, the main warehouse behind the street sales point. Johnson and Mason were the biggest importers of wine, sherry, port and spirits in the city, with extensive cellars underneath the building. Beyond it stands the Post Office, originally built for Cash's the silk weavers.

It is impossible to get far enough back to take an accurate view today. The Johnson & Mason building was replaced with the Bank Vaults in 1930 but the Post Office building survives, although sadly no longer a post office. Note that the top floor is gone; this was destroyed by fire on 14 November 1940.

LOOKING PAST THE Rover showroom towards Hertford Street in 1910. Next door stands the Three Tuns inn which stood here since at least the eighteenth century. Across the entrance to the barracks stands the Peeping Tom Hotel, hence Peeping Tom in the top window. He now graces a nook at the other end of the street. The tram is on its way to Coventry Station.

The same view today shows the Litten Tree on the site of the Rover showroom. This was previously Benley's, remembered by many for the varied range of goods it sold. Today the trees and flowers add a pleasant aspect to the area.

WARWICK ROW, ON the right, began to be built alongside the green in the early 1800s. What it overlooked was effectively a large area of rough grassland. In this photograph taken in the 1950s, beyond the statue of Sir Thomas White, is Stoneleigh Terrace, a grand row of Victorian houses demolished in the 1960s to build the ring road.

Most of the Georgian buildings thankfully survived, except for a small number that were demolished to make a road through the centre of the green. The statue of city benefactor Sir Thomas White remains. White, a London merchant, founded a charity in 1542, which continues to raise over £40,000 a year for charitable causes in Coventry.

GREYFRIAR'S GREEN, *c.* 1905. The siege cannon, dating from 1799, was captured during the Crimean War and was presented to the city in 1858 by Lord Cardigan. It was hit by a string of bombs in 1940 and scrapped in 1943. The green, being flatter in the past, was often used by the soldiers in the barracks for training purposes. Also, it was at one time a venue for Coventry's Great Fair.

The same view today but with many more trees and flowers. Although the old open flat green was nice, it cannot match today's green with its landscaping, if we ignore the road and the ring road – of course.

A RARE WINGRAVE showing the area around Coventry Station in the 1860s. The railway track can be seen running along the foreground, with two enclosures for loading cattle and sheep onto open carriages. To the left of them is a crane for lifting heavier goods. At this point, the railway had only been in the city about twenty-five years. Beyond is the classic south view of Coventry, with the tall Lombardy poplars.

The view today is not so inspiring. The building on the right however, the Rocket, still stands. This view is taken further forward than it should be, as the widening of the railway has made it impossible to get the exact prospect.

4

COOK STREET GATE TO BROADGATE

BROADGATE IN THE late 1950s. Godiva can be seen in the centre of her grassy island, and beyond stands Owen Owen. To the left are the Hotel Leofric and Broadgate House. Godiva has changed position and now faces forward.

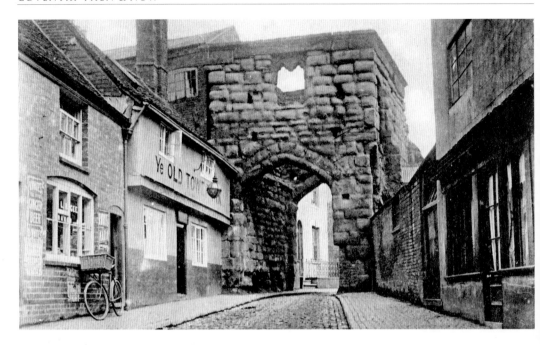

COOK STREET GATE in 1910, one of the city's minor gates. On the left stands the Old Tower Inn, which dated back to the Elizabethan period. When it closed, in an attempt to save it the brewery presented the inn to the city. The building was demolished in 1963.

Today the gate has noticeably had some basic restoration, including the return of its battlements. Outside the gate at one point in the past was a floodable ditch and a drawbridge. To the left now stands the British Legion Club and on the right Lady Herbert's Garden.

LADY HERBERT'S GARDEN and Cook Street Gate, photographed in the late 1930s. This area between the gates, known as the Rope Walk, was purchased by Sir Alfred Herbert to make a garden walk. His wife Florence, who initiated the idea, died suddenly in 1930 and Sir Alfred continued turning it into a memorial to his beloved wife. Florence's initials appear on all the uprights of the garden's bronze rails.

The garden remains relatively unchanged today and is well maintained by the city – still a haven of peace and beauty where once people lived and rope was made.

SWANSWELL GATE, *c.* 1910. When this photograph was taken it was a private residence, probably the strangest in the city apart the house in High Street which was less than 6ft wide and built in an old entry. The gate was converted into a private residence in the nineteenth century and soon after became a shop. It continued as a shop until 1930.

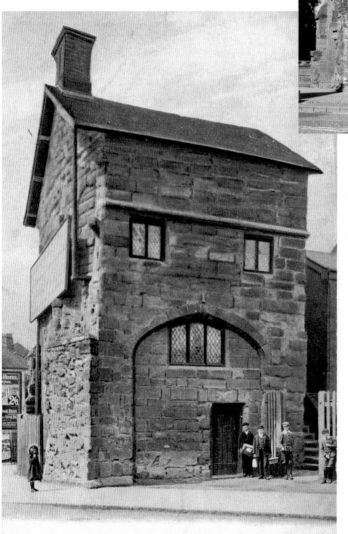

The gate was restored in 1931/2 by Sir Alfred Herbert as part of Lady Herbert's Garden. It has since been used as a shop more than once and is currently CV One.

A RARE VIEW showing the old and the new Hippodromes together in 1937. The old Hippodrome, built in 1907, was purchased in 1936 by Sir Alfred Herbert to extend Lady Herbert's Garden. The new Hippodrome opened on 1 November 1937, the day after the old one closed. Within months the old one was demolished. The new Hippodrome was demolished to build Millennium Place.

The same view today, showing part of Lady Herbert's Garden and Millennium Place. The blue glass bridge now crosses the garden, coming out beyond in a piece of 'garden', no doubt designed by an architect. This proves that gardens should always be designed by gardeners and not architects.

HALES STREET IN 1905. Swanswell Gate stands on the left, and on the right the fire station has not yet reached its full size. The building opened in 1902 and was manned by a voluntary force formed in 1861. The service became professional in 1934 and the fire station was extended by adding three more bays. Beyond can be seen Trinity Schools, with the small tower and spire.

The extra bays can now be seen. After remaining empty for many years, the fire station was turned into a bar and Indian restaurant. The foreground today is certainly different; on the right can be seen the controls for working the World Clock, which is set into the floor of Millennium Place.

THE CATTLE MARKET, left, and Hales Street, taken on the morning after the flood on 1 January 1900. Many woke up to extensive flooding, as if the ancient Babbu Lacu had reappeared, in some places over 6ft deep. For many a night of heavy rain, for others a nightmare. This area was once the Mill Dam, a sheet of water which lay here until the mid-nineteenth century.

The same scene today. The line of Hales Street goes directly behind the walking lady. Some of the buildings in Hales Street still stand but are hard to see because of the street furniture. The Transport Museum in the background now houses the largest collection of its type in the country, and is a first class museum which the city can be proud of.

HALES STREET IN 1905. On the right stands Mattersons, Huxley & Watsons, purveyors of agricultural instruments. Behind the cab is the Opera House, a popular place of entertainment including plays, musicals, opera, recitals and talks. One who spoke here was the famed Channel swimmer William Webb, also the great adventurer and survivor Sir Ernest Shackleton, who was also honoured in St Mary's Hall.

Much has changed today. The 1970s' building stands on the site of the Opera House behind the Grammar School. The end of the buildings on the left lie on the bend, behind the building on the left in the old view. In fact, nothing in the old photograph apart from the Grammar School has survived.

THE MILL DAM in 1829. It began life as part of the Babbu Lacu and is probably a remnant of St Osburg's Pool. This later shrunk further, forming two pools – one giving Pool Meadow its name. In medieval times the pool was utilised to run the Priory Mill. In 1840, the dam for the mill was finally removed and the water culverted. Drainage work finally cleared the land for building.

The view today should be looking slightly more to the right, but for the sake of a good picture of the Whittle Arch it has been lined up in the centre. Millennium Place has its raised World Clock, a trip hazard but good for keeping skateboarders at bay. Through the centre stands Sir Frank Whittle's statue and the entrance to Priory Place.

LOOKING UP FROM the Bull Ring into Butcher Row about 1905. On the right is the entrance to Little Butcher Row, and the road ahead up to the end of the pointed roof on the left is the Bull Ring, which takes its name from the fact that bulls were baited here from the fifteenth century. These buildings also lie across the site of the Gatehouse to the cathedral church of St Mary.

Today it's Trinity Street; all the buildings were demolished in 1936, hence what we see now. The Flying Standard was built in 1937 for Timothy Whites the Chemist, and covers the area on the old photograph up to the house with the pointed roof. Beyond is the flowerbed, previously Butcher Row. The Primark building, right, opened in 1954 as a replacement store for Owen Owen.

LOOKING DOWN BUTCHER Row in 1910. If it had survived, Butcher Row would have been one of the city's finest olde worlde streets. A fascinating mix of buildings dating back to the fifteenth century, Butcher Row began as in-fill outside the Priory gate and the large open area beyond. Markets were held here and eventually many of the stalls became permanent and the traders built shops here.

The same view today. The steps between the Flying Standard and the flowerbed are between the pointed roof, right, and the shop awning in the old photograph. Under the flowerbed and within 5 to 6ft of the front of the bed lie buried the cellars of the houses.

THE NUMBER 15 bus, photographed in the late 1950s, in Trinity Street used to run from Whitmore Park to Green Lane. These jump-on jump-off Daimlers are fondly remembered, with the driver encapsulated in the cabin and the conductor wandering about, 'Any more fares please!'

The modern equivalent, the number 13, up until recent years followed exactly the same route as the old number 15. The bus is a much bigger machine than the old one, capable of holding more passengers, and it still follows the old tradition of being a moving advertising board.

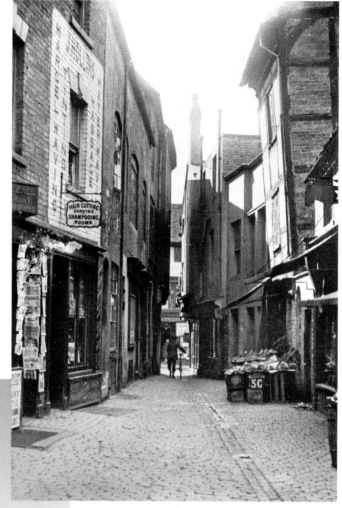

LOOKING DOWN LITTLE Butcher Row toward Cross Cheaping, *c.* 1905. As the cyclist leaves the lane at the bottom, the narrowness is particularly noticeable. It was once said that some of the lanes were so narrow that you could shake hands from opposing upper storey windows. The tall, sixteenth-century timbered building on the right was for many years called Ye Olde Curiosity Shoppe.

The view today holds nothing of interest. Primark stands on the left and West Orchards and other shops are ahead. Work began on the shopping complex in 1990 and it was built mainly on part of Smithford Way, a car park and service areas, so little of any interest was lost in its construction. It was named after the Prior's West Orchard, with no 's'.

AN EXCELLENT VIEW taken in the 1950s from Trinity churchyard, looking across Broadgate and framed by trees. Ahead, from right to left, can been seen Owen Owen, Broadgate House and the Bridge Restaurant straddling Hertford Street. In the centre of Broadgate was the grass island, with Godiva sitting majestically on her horse. No one saw her close up because no one went on the island.

Today those same trees still frame the view, although now it is a little more cluttered with the bus shelters in the foreground and Cathedral Lanes on the left. It is, however, still the same bustling area and still represents the heart of the city.

COVENTRY CROSS, STANDING at the meeting point of Cross Cheaping and Broadgate. The name Cross Cheaping means the cross in the market place, and Broadgate refers to the entrance to Coventry Castle at the top/left of Broadgate. The Coventry Cross was once one of the finest in the land, standing 57ft high; covered in gold leaf, it shimmered in the sunlight.

A scaled-down copy of the Coventry Cross today, next to Holy Trinity Church. To the left of the cross here in 1849 Mary Ball, the last person executed in Coventry, was hanged before thousands. She still lies buried deep down to the left of the cross in what was the old gaol's exercise yard.

HUGELY CHANGED SINCE Wingrave photographed it in the 1860s, this view, taken in the 1930s, gives one a sense of the later, wider Broadgate. Broadgate pre-early nineteenth century wouldn't have been that much wider than the width of the bank. In this view we see the Burton's building (right) then the King's Head, with Peeping Tom in the top corner niche, and, opposite, an unchanged National Westminster Bank.

Broadgate today, vastly improved since the tent was removed last year. Although this scene is modern, the site of Broadgate is very ancient, for here in the past have been found Roman coins, and within a few feet of where this photograph was taken, a Bronze Age axe head dating to 350 BC was dug up. A second from the spoil was later discovered.

5

HERE & THERE

ST THOMAS'S CHURCH in the Butts, as it appeared in the 1860s. This nineteenth-century church was built mainly for the watchmakers of this growing suburb. It was badly damaged during the war and was finally demolished in the early 1970s. A block of flats now stands on the site.

PANSY MONTAGUE, KNOWN by her stage name as 'La Milo', was the choice for Lady Godiva in 1907. Here she is seen riding down a packed Much Park Street, buried in the biggest wig known to man or woman. Despite this, Canon Beaumont described her attire as 'unspeakably Vulgar'. The procession was seen by 150,000 people and took five hours to complete its course. On the left is Much Park Gate.

The Godiva for 2010 was unusually a model; not a model like in the past, but literally a model. Here the white lady is seen passing by the front of the Council House, covered in giant butterflies! If we also added a black figure on horseback we would have the equivalent of the old Southam Godiva processions.

PART OF A procession in the late 1950s with a ladies' and girls' marching kazoo band passing through Broadgate. The processions of the 1950s, including the Coventry Carnival procession, were huge and went on for hours, with hundreds of large floats sponsored by the city's main manufacturers.

The Godiva Procession of 2010, with a band marching along the same piece of Broadgate. The modern processions are much smaller and do not have the same back-up or funding as yesteryear but still, thankfully, someone is trying to keep up the old traditions.

PROBABLY THE 1929 procession, which concentrated on a historical theme. Two gents dressed as seventeenth-century characters and one dressed as Henry VIII stand at the end of the procession in the Memorial Park. This was, and still is, the ending point of all Godiva Processions. In the past it held events and a fair, today the much admired Godiva Festival.

Not quite historical characters but a group of colourful floats of monsters, sea life and animals, passing through the streets in the Godiva Procession of 2010.

A FLOAT MADE by members of the Coventry and District Co-operative Society for the Godiva Procession of 1936, showing Cleopatra on her golden galley with her handmaidens, Mark Anthony, Caesar and Roman soldiers. At the end of the procession, 100,000 gathered in the Memorial Park where this photograph was taken.

Colourful floats pass by the new and old cathedrals in the 2010 procession.

THE ORIGINAL FIGURE of Peeping Tom in the yard of the King's Head, photographed in the 1860s. Newly painted and wearing his cockade hat ready for the Godiva Procession, the fifteenth-century figure is thought to be an image of St George. His arms had been cut off so he could peep from windows back in 1659.

The same figure today looks out of Cathedral Lanes, appropriately over the statue of Lady Godiva in Broadgate. His back is slightly hollowed out, as in the past splinters of George were sold or given as souvenirs. Such images are a rare survival from the past and our George is an exceptional one.

BLACK SWAN TERRACE in Spon End, photographed around 1900. This six-cottage terrace, built by Coventry Priory in 1454, has a long and varied history. The end two cottages were later made into one; No. 123 the became Black Swan tavern. It was frequented by Mary Ann Higgins, who was hanged for the murder of her Uncle William Higgins in 1831.

The terrace was expertly restored by the Spon End Building Preservation Trust between 1998 and 2007. Number 122 has been reverted back to how it looked in 1540 and is now used to demonstrate the life of a weaving family in sixteenth-century Coventry.

PARK JAMES COTTAGE on the corner of Cow Lane and Cheylesmore in 1929. James was the keeper of the Gardens and Cheylesmore Estate. The building above was the original Hare & Squirrel, then run by Arthur Petty. It was from this inn that farmer Thomas Edwards from Stoneleigh was followed and attacked by two soldiers and a weaver, who, after they died, were hanged and gibbeted on Gibbet Hill in 1765.

The later rebuilt Hare & Squirrel from the 1930s stands to the right and is now simply The Squirrel. Nothing survives of the sixteenth-century buildings; they were demolished and their ancient timbers burnt back in the 1930s.

THE COURTYARD OF Ford's Hospital in Greyfriar's Lane, *c.* 1910. The hospital was founded in 1509 by William Ford, and his father William Pisford Senior enlarged the endowment. William Pisford stated in his will that it should house six aged men and their wives being over sixty years of age, of good name, in poverty and living in Coventry. He also willed that a priest lived with them and said mass for the founders and the inmates. By the eighteenth century the hospital had become exclusively female, housing in 1817 seventeen aged women with their own rooms.

The hospital was partially blown up by a bomb on 14 October 1940, killing the warden, a nurse and six inmates. It was restored mainly by builder and historian Abe Jephcot and re-opened in 1953. The courtyard was gated for the first time in 500 years about eight years ago, when teenagers began worrying the residents. Today the building houses both men and women.

CHEYLESMORE GATE AND Manor House, *c*. 1890. The Earl of Arundel is believed to have built the original manor house in 1237. On the death of Queen Isabella it passed to Edward the Black Prince, then to Richard II, who had the city wall diverted to encompass it. The gatehouse at the time of this photograph being taken was a single residence; it was later split into two cottages.

The manor left royal hands when Charles II gave it to Sir Thomas Townsend, who lived in it until 1685. The building was restored to its present condition in 1965 and is the city's Registry Office. Although much of the present building dates from the seventeenth century, parts still date back to the fourteenth century. The actual hall itself survived the war converted into tenements, and was demolished in 1955.

THE CHAPEL OF St Christopher and St James at the beginning of the Second World War. Note the tree and bollards, painted white because of the blackout. The chapel was built outside of Spon Gate to give refuge to travellers who arrived at the city after the gates had closed. Here they could spend the night in safety and say a prayer to the dedicated saints, both favoured by travellers.

The chapel took minor damage during the war and needed little restoration. It was, however, decided by the then city council to demolish it and turn it into a 'picturesque' ruin. During the rebuilding of the city in the 1950s, few in the council thought of the past or wanted to think of the past; to them the future was all-important.

THE OLD GRAMMAR School in 1859. Looking from Bishop Street, it depicts the building in the eighteenth century when it was still in use as a school. The pillared gates led into open

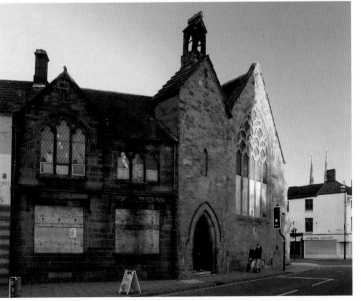

ground used by the pupils for recreation. Above the tower hangs the bell which summoned the children to school. This engraving also shows the later, probably sixteenth century, timbered wing of the building, which amongst other things housed the library.

Today the building remains boarded up, as it has done for a number of years. Note that Hales Street now passes straight through the timbered wing; its cellar still runs under the road.

THE SCHOOL OF Art and Holy Trinity Schools on the corner of Ford and Hales Street, *c.* 1910. The school in the background was opened in 1854 and was partially built with stones from the city wall, which formed the southern boundary of the site. The art school, built in Gothic style, was opened by Sir Joseph Paxton in 1863, paid for by public subscription.

Today nothing survives except some of the carvings of craftsmen at work, which adorned the tops of the arches of the School of Art. These are stored away in one of the city's stores. The buildings did survive the bombs but fell to planners. The area on the left is now the modernised Pool Meadow bus station.

A COVENTRY POLICEMAN stands outside the Old Watch House in the Market Square in the 1860s. The 1835 Municipal Corporation Act made it law that every borough should have its own police force. Coventry already had an unpaid force led by Thomas Henry Prosser, an ex-Bow Street Runner. In 1836 its first paid force consisted of Prosser, an inspector, a sergeant and twenty constables.

In 1969, the Coventry force was amalgamated and became the Warwickshire and Coventry Constabulary. In 1974, changes in political boundaries forced the Coventry force to become part of West Midlands Police. Outside the main station in Little Park Street, opened in 1957, stand PS Caren Fletcher and PS Adrian Murray. Coventry's police force is as dedicated today as it has always been protecting the people of Coventry. These are true local heroes.

LITTLE PARK STREET on 15 November 1940. The street was devastated with bombs and incendiaries. At times on that night it was said that the street was an impassable wall of fire. City historian and archaeologist John Bailey Shelton spent the night trying to save his horses and his museum, which stood in the street. His bravery that night won him a medal from the RSPCA.

The road today, more leafy, has an odd quiet moment; nothing has survived of the old street. It's hard to believe the fireball that engulfed this street on the night of 14 November 1940 now leaves no trace. After the main blitz, many homeless people, including Shelton, lived in caravans to the left of the picture.

'HAPPY MUCH PARK', as Drayton the poet wrote in the late sixteenth century, was not a happy place after 14 November. The driver of this car was killed after he crashed into the bomb crater. Much of the street did, however, survive to be pulled down by planners, who over the years put nothing of interest back in their place.

The street today has little to commend it, except for the gatehouse and the stone remains of the merchants' houses exposed by the bombs. It's hard to believe that this was the main entrance into the city from the London Road, and was once lined with some of the city's best houses. This photograph was in fact taken in 2009, as at the time of writing it was impossible to get the view due to building work.

A COVENTRY HACKNEY carriage driver with his two legged horse! Only joking. These carriages or cabs, which were entered from the front, plied the streets of the city from picking-up points in Broadgate, Hales Street and at the end of Hertford Street. Much the same as today.

An LTC Coventry-built taxi cab today. Known the world over, it has become a British icon, as was the old Coventry-built Daimler bus.

TRAMS AT THE junction of Hales, Ford and Jesson Street in 1899. These open-top trams belonging to the Coventry Electrical Tramway Company, had superseded the earlier steam-powered tram back in 1895. These electric-powered trams, which picked up their power via the rods and cables, proved much quieter and more reliable than their steam-powered predecessors.

The same view today; none of the houses survive and none of the city's trams except tram number 71, which ran along the Stoke route. The bottom half of this 1930/1 tram was used for a number of years as a garden shed in Surrey. It is presently under restoration.

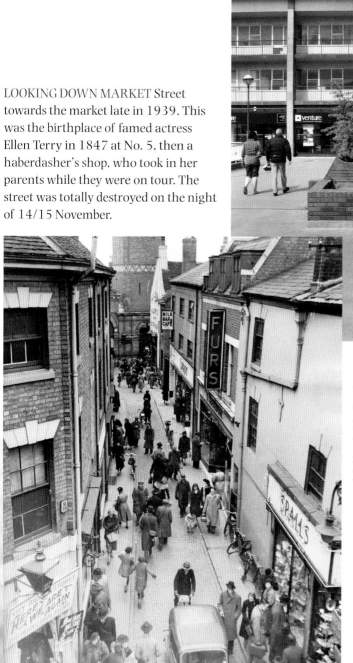

LOOKING DOWN MARKET Street towards the market late in 1939. This was the birthplace of famed actress Ellen Terry in 1847 at No. 5, then a haberdasher's shop, who took in her parents while they were on tour. The street was totally destroyed on the night of 14/15 November.

Taken from the same vantage point today, we find ourselves at the top of the ramp in the Upper Precinct. On the wall ahead is a blue plaque recording the birth of Dame Ellen Terry near this spot.

A BUSY SCENE in the Market Place in 1910. On the left is the Market Hall and Fish Market, and beyond is the entrance into West Orchard. The pub on the right was the Market Tavern, which was run by the author's great aunt; it was also known as the Hole in the Wall from a cartoon which hung over the bar. The area was destroyed on 14/15 November and later a market stood here, until the rebuilding in the early 1950s.

The market today; a colourful, busy, bustling place full of all sorts, from fruit to fishing tackle to picture frames. The building is currently protected by English Heritage because of its unusual round shape.

THE MARTYRS' MEMORIAL near the junction of Mile Lane and Quinton Road in 1929. The memorial, which commemorates the burning of eleven religious martyrs, was unveiled in 1910. It stood about 200 yards from the Park Hollows, Cheylesmore, where the burnings took place.

Although the memorial gives the impression of being in the same place, it was in fact moved a short distance during the construction of the ringroad, and now stands at the top of Little Park Street in the middle of a roundabout.

PROBABLY THE STEEPEST point in the centre of Coventry is the old cobbled lane leading up to Hill Top in Priory Row. The photograph was taken in the 1930s, but the scene hasn't changed since Victorian times. Many of Coventry's lanes and streets were cobbled with river stones in the past.

The same view today, still relatively unchanged apart from a couple of new entrances and walls. This lane actually cuts through the transepts of the city's long-lost cathedral.

6

AROUND THE SUBURBS

A NINETEENTH-CENTURY engraving of Allesley Hall and park. Thomas Flynt built the hall in 1660 in front of the site of the old castle. In 1692, Henry Neale purchased the estate and greatly added to the hall.

NEW HOUSE, KERESLEY, as it appeared in 1703. Surely the most handsome house in Coventry, built on the site of the Bishop of Coventry's hunting grange by John Hales, nephew of John Hales of Whitefriars. Completed in 1586, it was walled with many formal gardens and statues. It was also home to the Burnabys, Yelvertons and Bohuns. This beautiful house, with its 150 windows, was demolished in 1778.

The scene today, from the corner of Keresley Road and Sadler Road. New House stood behind this block of flats, built just forward of the old moated grange. The grass area across the foreground and running across the road to the left is called New House Green, although few today know this.

KERESLEY CHURCH OF England School was opened in 1852. Built in the medieval style, its tower originally had a short umbrella spire upon it. In 1859 it held sixty-five boys and ninety girls. The school itself was based upstairs in a large, open room; the schoolmaster lived downstairs. It served the local community for ninety-two years and was finally closed and sold in 1962, and later demolished.

The site today is covered by a large but low block of flats, almost hidden behind the trees. In the distance can be seen the spire of the church which was once associated with the old school. This corner was once the site of the Keresley gallows, and during the war the green triangle of Keresley Heath was also the site of a barrage balloon.

THE NUGGET INN, Coundon Green Road, in 1936. Its story, probably one of the most unusual in the city, says it was purchased with a golden nugget brought back from the California Gold Rush. Others say it was a nugget from the Australian gold rush. Whichever it was, as a tale it is not impossible. In 1858 a beer house here was owned by Thomas Green.

Today we see a later Golden Nugget pub, built in the 1930s and with some nice deco style features. The site of the original Nugget was around the corner, where the first house is. Coundon Green is still a pleasant area and is also home to Coundon School, once home of George Singer of cycle and car fame.

RADFORD VILLAGE EARLY in the twentieth century, when still semi-rural. On the left, up a cobbled bank, stands a row of weavers' cottages, built probably in the early nineteenth century. Beyond them on the rising bank are more cottages and the Buck & Crown Inn, one of two pubs in the village. On the right stands Radford House, and beyond is Warden's Farm, where the children queued for their treat on Curds & Wey Sunday. This was once a vibrant little village, with baptisms in the local spring, ponies running wild across the common and prize fights.

Today nothing survives. The first row of cottages did make it through until the 1970s, but are now a car wash. The rising area can still be seen, minus its buildings. That said it is now a green, home to the war memorial dedicated to those Radford lads who gave their lives for freedom. Aldi (right) is built on land that once fronted Warden's Farm, and the flats were built on Radford House.

THE ORIGINAL GRAPES Inn on the Radford Road towards Barr's Hill, photographed around 1910. It is said that one regular visitor would spend the afternoon in the inn, drink all he could, then clamber onto the back of his cart and instantly fall asleep, knowing his horse would safely return him home. Could that be his horse and cart outside?

The same view today; the present Grapes pub stands opposite, built in the 1930s. The houses here were all built in the early 1930s; one house on the corner still has a wall, part of the old Grapes, standing 8ft tall against its side.

A RARE, LATE nineteenth-century view of St Catherine's Well standing amongst the fields. Stories behind this well are highly suggestible that it is of ancient origins and sacred. In the early 1400s, the present well head and structure was built by the Priory of St Mary. Up until 1847 the well supplied the Spon End area with up to 100,000 gallons of water a day.

Today, in the curve of Beaumont Crescent, the well remains a survivor of Coventry's medieval past set within a row of 1930s' houses. Much of the base area, although it looks old, was added in sandstone in 1935. When this work was done, workmen unearthed the remains of a small stone rectangular building. Beyond this, in the 1830s, Radford Horse Races took place.

A NAVAL GUN being taken by rail across the Stoney Stanton Road from the Ordnance Works in 1914. Coventry Ordnance Works in Red Lane cast a vast number of huge guns during the First World War. Tested in huge pits, some fired shells up to 22 miles. The works, which produced field guns and munitions, closed in 1922. Its existence was responsible for the growth of housing in the area.

The shaded area in the foreground is the exact point where the gun in the old picture is crossing the road; the railway track which linked up to the main line is now gone. The taller houses on the right now stand lower as the weaver's top shops with the large windows have since been removed.

BROWNING ROAD, STOKE, in the 1930s. Desirable two-bayed residences for the new house buyer, probably costing between £300 and £400. There are three cars in the street, no television aerials and one street light.

Browning Road today, relatively unchanged except for the television aerials, telephone posts and cars – lots of them.

A LOVELY VIEW of the old horse pond at Stoke Green, *c.* 1910. Notice the slipway on the left, down which farmers took their wagons into the water to tighten their wheels. The Stoke Green area was mainly first settled in the seventeenth century, when many fairly wealthy individuals lived here, including, for a short time during the Civil War, Parliamentary politician, John Pym.

Today, it is still a pleasant prospect but lacking the water which seemed to add so much more to the previous scene. The site of the old pool was later turned into a paddling pool but has since reverted back to grass, it being too expensive to maintain.

HEARSALL COMMON, *c.* 1910. This area in the past was a larger wooded area with a stretch of open sandy moorland covered in bushes, gorse, grasses and heather. In the early twentieth century it was still home to the sand lizard, grass snake and adder. It was a favoured walking place for the Victorians. The common also once was home to a windmill and venue for prize fights.

Today the same view, now well shorn. The common once held grazing rights for the city's freemen. These rights were reduced in 1860 and 1875, and finally ended in 1927 so freemen no longer hold any right to graze cattle here. This part of the common gained its present flat form during the 1860s, when unemployed weavers were put to work levelling part of it and Whitley Common.

THE GROVE IN the 1930s. Known locally as the 'Stump' it was a raised grove of trees, which stood in the centre of the original village of Stivichall. All that remains of this is a rebuilt church, Stivichall Grange and Bremont College, which is believed to have been the village's original manor house.

Today it is basically unchanged, except for the modern trappings of street furniture, traffic lights etc. Beyond lies the Memorial Park, opened in October 1927 by Field-Marshal Haig, a living memorial to our war dead with the cenotaph in the centre.

LOOKING FROM THE Kenilworth Road towards the Grove in 1920. Although first mentioned by its name in 1313, the road is in fact older and is the road to Kenilworth, cleared of close vegetation by Simon de Montfort in the twelfth century to stop robberies.

The same view today, although less peaceful due to modern traffic noise. The Grove ahead still has trees; pines – often associated with stopping places for drovers. The Grove itself (middle right) may have early prehistoric origins, as much of this area up to Gibbet Hill was extensively occupied in the prehistoric period.

COAT OF ARMS Bridge Road, photographed around 1910. Past huge ancient oaks and down the dirt road stands a fine bridge bearing the arms of the Gregory family, who owned the estate up until 1928. The lane was originally called Cock's Lane until the bridge was built by the London & North Western Railway in 1844.

Today, although still a pleasant spot, the loss of the old oaks and the addition of tarmac and paving seem to take much away from the rusticity and beauty of the old view. That said, the area still forms visually one of the pleasanter parts of the city.

COAT OF ARMS Bridge from the other side, taken after 1932. By the bridge can be seen a small timbered cottage, and in the right foreground a larger, later brick cottage standing by the memorial, which reminds us that Stivichall Estate was presented to the city by Major Charles Hugh Gregory-Hood in 1932.

Today the scene is relatively unchanged. The railings no longer surround the memorial, having disappeared during the Second World War in a scrappage scheme. Nearby once stood the blacksmith's shop, which was still in business well into the twentieth century.

THE REMAINS OF Caludon Castle, photographed around 1940. Stephen de Seagrave died in 1241 leaving a manor house here. In 1305 it was fortified and moated, and in 1354 it was rebuilt and extended. Around 1530, Lord Berkeley rebuilt much of the castle. Its most famous resident, if we choose to believe local tradition, was St George, who was said to have been born here.

Today little has changed except the castle ruins no longer stand amongst farmers' fields; now it stand in a public area attached to Caludon Castle School. Still in good condition, the ruinous remains once formed the end of the castle's Great Hall.

CHILDREN STANDING NEAR the war memorial in Walsgrave, *c*. 1925. Originally called 'Sowa', the Walsgrave part was added later and may indicate a burial mound or sacred grove. After the Conquest it was held by Richard the Huntsman. In the thirteenth century, Hugh de Loges held it on the condition that he presented the Earl of Chester with a barbed arrow so he could kill a deer on passing.

Many of the old cottages survive, except for the top two in Hall Lane. The one on the right of the old photograph was the Shoulder of Mutton Inn. In the foreground now stands the Ansty Road, a dual carriageway. Originally less than half its present width, it was a quiet track leading to Hinckley. Walsgrave was still a village up to the Second World War.

BINLEY TOLL GATE on the Binley Road, *c.* 1905. This eighteenth-century tollgate actually stood in Stoke, and those who passed through, except those on foot, had to pay a fee. The keeper in the eighteenth century, Charles Pinchbeck, was shot through the hand and robbed by two villains from Brinklow. He later died and the two men who killed him were hanged above the toll gate in 1773.

Not the quiet lane of old but the multi-lanes of the junction of Binley Road and Hipswell Highway. The toll house stood about 50ft up from the present road junction and survived into the 1960s.

WHITLEY MILL AND Whitley Bridge, *c.* 1905. The mill stood here for centuries into the twentieth century. It, and the eighteenth-century bridge, stood on the original route of the London Road, which was changed to its present course for coaches in 1826-7. This stretch of the original London Road over the bridge afterwards became Abbey Road.

Today the bridge is still there but there is no mill. The mill, said to be haunted, survived until the 1960s or '70s. Abbey Road, in pre-coaching days, was known locally as The Hollow Way. This relates to when it was a prehistoric sunken track which led to a prehistoric fort covering part of Whitley Common, all signs of which disappeared when it was levelled in the nineteenth century.

Other titles published by The History Press

Haunted Coventry

DAVID MCGRORY

Within the pages of this book you will find the Phantom Monk of Priory Row, ghostly Grey Ladies, a spectre that appears to do the washing up, a phantom lorry, and the Devil himself, rattling chains at Whitefriars – just a taste of the many restless spirits to be found in haunted Coventry. From spectres in the suburbs to haunted pubs, this chilling collection of strange sightings in the city is sure to appeal to everyone intrigued by Coventry's haunted heritage.

978 0 7524 3708 8

Coventry's Motorcycle Heritage

DAMIEN KIMBERLEY

From the first velocipedes built in 1868, most of the later well-established cycle manufacturers quickly turned their attention to motorised vehicles, and many of the early motoring pioneers moved to Coventry to become part of this revolutionary work. From world-famous companies like Triumph, to the more obscure marques like Wartnaby and Draper, this book provides a brief summary of each manufacturer, as well as an insight into the social history of Coventry at the peak of its involvement in motorcycle history.

978 0 7509 5125 8

Birmingham Then & Now

MARK NORTON

Take a nostalgic visual journey back to 1960s Birmingham to witness the much-loved Bull Ring, the grand city-centre buildings that were demolished to make way for the 'modern' city, and the streets and courts that were swept away during the last fifty years of development. Mark Norton presents many previously unpublished pictures alongside his own colour photographs of the area in the twenty-first century. Thoughtful and detailed captions provide a new insight into the ever-changing city.

978 0 7524 5722 2

Birmingham: A History in Maps

PAUL LESLIE LINE

From the exceptional town plans and maps contained within this unique volume emerges a social picture of Birmingham, a town quickly developing in size and population in the eighteenth century, along with the changes brought about by urbanisation. Accompanied with informative text and pictures of the cityscape, the many detailed plans contained in this historic atlas of Birmingham are a gateway to its past, allowing the reader and researcher to visually observe the journey of this historic town to city status in 1889 and beyond.

978 0 7524 6089 5

Visit our website and discover thousands of other History Press books.

www.thehistorypress.co.uk